Just like my

Mother used

to Bake

Just like my
Mother used
to *Bake*

RYLAND
PETERS
& SMALL

LONDON NEW YORK

Senior designer Toni Kay

Senior editor Catherine Osborne

Picture research Emily Westlake

Production Gordana Simakovic

Art director Leslie Harrington

Publishing director Alison Starling

Notes

All spoon measurements are level unless otherwise specified.

All eggs are medium unless otherwise specified. Uncooked or partly cooked eggs should not be served to the very young, the very old, those with compromised immune systems, or to pregnant women.

Ovens should be preheated to the specified temperature. If using a fan-assisted oven, cooking times should be reduced according to the manufacturer's instructions.

First published in the United States in 2008 by Ryland Peters & Small, Inc.
519 Broadway, 5th Floor
New York, NY 10012
www.rylandpeters.com

Text copyright © Fiona Beckett, Susannah Blake, Maxine Clark, Linda Collister, Brian Glover, Clare Gordon-Smith, Rachael Anne Hill, Fran Warde, and Ryland Peters & Small 2008 (*see* page 64 for details). Design and photography copyright © Ryland Peters & Small 2008.

10 9 8 7 6 5 4 3 2 1

ISBN: 978-1-84597-600-2

Printed and bound in China

Contents

Perfect Bakes

Who can resist the smell of a freshly baked apple pie pulled straight from the oven? When it comes to traditional bakes, mothers are the experts. Many of us will remember weekends spent in the kitchen helping cook batches of deliciously sweet cupcakes for friends and family. There's certainly nothing quite like a mother's guiding hand in the kitchen.

For those of you who long to recreate those bakes from childhood, the recipes in this book will have you whipping up irresistible chocolate chip cookies in no time. Why not make a batch for your mother, or bake with her just like old times? A celebration of mothers everywhere, *Just Like My Mother Used to Bake* is a delectable collection of homemade cakes, pies, tarts, and cookies.

Fruity Bakes

For the best results, always use a metal pie pan: it will get hotter than ceramic and guarantees to cook the pie crust until dry and crumbly rather than soggy.

Blackberry and apple pie

1 RECIPE SWEET SHORTCRUST PASTRY DOUGH (*SEE* PAGE 62)

1½ lb. baking apples, cored, peeled, and sliced

1 lb. blackberries, about 3½ cups

milk, for brushing

sugar, for sprinkling

custard, to serve

a metal pie pan, 10 inches diameter, lightly buttered

SERVES 6

Preheat the oven to 425°F. Remove 1 piece of chilled dough from the refrigerator and roll out until just larger than the pie pan. Put the rolled dough into the pie pan, pressing the base and rim gently to push out any air bubbles. Layer the apple slices, blackberries, and sugar over the dough, piling the fruit high, then brush milk over the dough rim.

Roll out the remaining dough to just bigger than the dish and drape it over the fruit, taking care not to stretch it. Trim the excess dough away from the edge and then go around the rim of the pie, pinching the dough together with your fingers to seal. Using a small, sharp knife, cut a vent in the middle of the pie to let the steam escape.

Brush the top of the pie all over with milk and sprinkle generously with sugar. Bake in the preheated oven for 30 minutes, then reduce to 350°F and cook for about another 30 minutes until golden. Serve hot with custard.

Mixed berry tartlets

These delightfully fruity tarts are perfect as little snacks or as a tangy treat—refreshing on the palate, they are sure to satisfy any sweet tooth.

To make the dough, put the flours, butter, and orange zest in a food processor and blend for 1 to 2 minutes until the mixture resembles bread crumbs. With the machine running, gradually pour 3 to 4 tablespoons cold water through the feed tube until the mixture forms a ball. Transfer the dough to a lightly floured counter and knead it until smooth and pliable. Wrap and chill in the refrigerator for 30 minutes.

Preheat the oven to 400°F. Roll out the dough thinly on a lightly floured counter. Using the cookie cutter, cut out 12 rounds and line the tartlet pans with them. Prick the bases lightly with a fork, then put a small piece of crumpled foil in each one. Bake in the preheated oven for 12 minutes. Remove the foil and return the pastry cases to the oven for another 3 to 5 minutes until the pastry is cooked. Remove from the oven and let cool before filling.

To make the filling, cut any large fruit in half. Put the crème fraîche or yogurt and orange zest in a bowl and mix. Spoon it into the tartlet crusts and put the fruit on top. Sprinkle with a little confectioners' sugar and serve immediately.

DOUGH

¾ cup white flour, plus extra for dusting

¾ cup whole-wheat flour

6½ tablespoons unsalted butter, chilled and cut into small pieces

1 tablespoon finely grated unwaxed orange zest

BERRY FILLING

2 pints mixed summer berries, including blueberries, strawberries, and raspberries, hulled

1¼ cups crème fraîche or thick yogurt

1 tablespoon finely grated unwaxed orange zest

2 teaspoons confectioners' sugar

a cookie cutter, 3 inches diameter

12 small tartlet pans

MAKES 12

This is a tart filled with an uncooked lemon curd and baked in the oven until just firm. A refreshingly decadent bake, ideal for a lazy summer afternoon sweet treat.

Classic lemon tart

1 RECIPE SWEET RICH SHORTCRUST PASTRY DOUGH (*SEE* PAGE 56)

1 egg, beaten

sour cream or crème fraîche, to serve (optional)

LEMON FILLING

6 extra large eggs

2⅓ cups sugar

finely grated zest and strained juice of 4 juicy unwaxed lemons

1¼ sticks unsalted butter, melted

a false-bottom fluted tart pan, 9 inches diameter

SERVES 8

Bring the dough to room temperature. Preheat the oven to 400°F. Roll out the dough thinly on a lightly floured work surface, and use to line the tart pan. Chill or freeze for 15 minutes, then bake blind following the method given on page 61. Brush with the beaten egg, then bake again for 5–10 minutes until set and shiny—this will prevent the filling from making the crust soggy.

Turn the oven down to 300°F. To make the lemon filling, put the eggs, sugar, lemon zest and juice, and butter into a food processor and blend until smooth.

Set the baked pie crust on a baking sheet and pour in the filling. Bake in the oven for about 1 hour (it may need a little longer, depending on your oven), until just set. Remove from the oven and let cool completely before serving.

Serve at room temperature, maybe with a spoonful of sour cream or crème fraîche, if using.

This fruity treat is made all the more naughty with the addition of whipping cream.

Victoria sandwich
with strawberries and cream

Preheat the oven to 350°F. Beat together the butter and sugar in a large bowl until pale and fluffy. Beat in the eggs, one at a time. Sift the flour into the mixture and fold in until thoroughly combined.

Spoon the cake mixture into the prepared pans and spread out evenly using the back of a spoon. Bake in the preheated oven for 20–25 minutes until golden brown and the cake springs back when pressed gently with the tips of your fingers. Turn out the cakes onto a wire rack, gently peel off the lining paper, and let cool completely.

To serve, slice a thin sliver off the top of one of the cakes to create a flat surface. Spread with the strawberry jam and top with the strawberries. Whip the cream until it stands in soft peaks, then spread on top of the strawberries. Top with the second cake, press down gently and dust with confectioners' sugar.

6 oz. butter, at room temperature

¾ cup plus 2 tablespoons sugar

3 eggs

1½ cups self-rising flour

3½ tablespoons good-quality strawberry jam

1 cup strawberries, hulled and halved or quartered, depending on size

½ cup whipping cream

confectioners' sugar, for dusting

two 8-inch cake pans with removable bottoms, greased and base-lined with parchment paper

SERVES 8

A tart that celebrates the perfect marriage of raspberries and cream. This is simplicity itself to make, but must be assembled at the last moment to keep the freshness and crispness of the crust. Sweeten the cream with a little strained homemade raspberry jam and add a dash of framboise (raspberry liqueur) if you have it.

1 RECIPE PÂTE BRISÉE (*SEE* PAGE 58)

2–3 tablespoons homemade raspberry jam

2¼ cups heavy cream, or 1¼ cups heavy cream mixed with 1¼ cups crème fraîche or sour cream

2 tablespoons framboise (optional)

1½ lb. fresh raspberries (5 cups)

1¼ cups raspberry or red currant jelly (any berry jelly will do)

a false-bottom fluted tart pan, 8 inches diameter

SERVES 6–8

Fresh raspberry tart

Bring the dough to room temperature. Preheat the oven to 400°F. Roll out the dough thinly on a lightly floured work surface, and use to line the tart pan. Prick the base, chill or freeze for 15 minutes, then bake blind following the method given on page 61. Let cool.

Press the raspberry jam through a strainer to remove the seeds, then put into a large bowl. Add the cream and framboise, if using. Beat until thick and just holding peaks. Spoon into the pie crust and level the surface. Cover with the raspberries, arranging a final neat layer on top.

Put the raspberry or red currant jelly into a small saucepan and warm it gently until liquid. Brush over the raspberries to glaze. Put into the refrigerator to chill and set for 10 minutes only before serving (no longer or the tart will become soggy).

Indulgent Treats

Some brownie enthusiasts believe that only cocoa should be used, not melted chocolate, as it gives a deeper, truly intense chocolate flavor.

Old-fashioned brownies

1 cup walnut pieces

4 extra large eggs

1½ cups superfine sugar

1¼ sticks butter, melted

½ teaspoon pure vanilla extract

1 cup plus 2 tablespoons all-purpose flour

¼ cup unsweetened cocoa powder

a brownie pan, 8 x 10 inches, greased and base-lined with parchment paper

MAKES 16

Preheat the oven to 325°F. Put the walnut pieces in an ovenproof dish and lightly toast in the oven for about 10 minutes. Leave to cool. Don't turn off the oven.

Meanwhile, break the eggs into a mixing bowl. Use an electric hand-mixer to whisk until frothy, then whisk in the sugar. Whisk for a minute, then, still whisking constantly, add the melted butter in a steady stream. Whisk for a minute more, then whisk in the vanilla. Sift the flour and cocoa into the bowl and stir in using a wooden spoon. When thoroughly combined, stir in the nuts. Transfer the mixture to the prepared pan and spread evenly.

Bake in the preheated oven for about 25 minutes until a skewer inserted halfway between the sides and the center comes out just clean. Remove the pan from the oven. Let cool completely before removing the brownie from the pan and cutting into 16 pieces. Store in an airtight container and eat within 5 days.

Coffee and walnut cake

This teatime classic feels like a little piece of childhood —bringing back memories of afternoon visits from grandmas and great-aunts.

Preheat the oven to 350°F. Beat together the butter and sugar in a large bowl until pale and fluffy, then beat in the eggs one at a time. Sift the flour into the butter mixture and fold in, then fold in the nuts and dissolved coffee. Divide between the prepared cake pans and spread out evenly. Bake in the preheated oven for 20–25 minutes until golden and the cake springs back when pressed gently with the tips of your fingers. Turn the cakes out onto a wire rack, carefully peel off the lining paper, and let cool completely.

To make the coffee frosting, warm the cream and coffee in a small saucepan, stirring until the coffee has dissolved. Pour into a bowl, add the butter, and sift the confectioners' sugar into the mixture. Beat together until smooth.

To serve, slice a thin sliver off the top of one of the cakes to create a flat surface. Spread with slightly less than half of the coffee frosting, then place the second cake on top. Spread the remaining frosting on top and decorate with walnut halves.

6 oz. butter, at room temperature

¼ cup plus 2 tablespoons sugar

3 eggs

1½ cups self-rising flour

⅓ cup walnut pieces

2 teaspoons instant coffee, dissolved in 1 tablespoon boiling water

walnut halves, to decorate

COFFEE FROSTING

2 tablespoons cream

2 teaspoons instant coffee

3½ oz. butter, at room temperature

1 scant cup confectioners' sugar

two 8-inch cake pans with removable bottoms, greased and base-lined with parchment paper

SERVES 5–6

The lightest and airiest of all sponge cakes, filled with crème fraîche and raspberries. Blueberries are a delicious alternative, if preferred.

Hazelnut roulade

6 eggs

¼ cup plus 1 tablespoon sugar, plus extra for sprinkling

¼ cup plus 1 tablespoon self-rising flour, sifted

½ cup hazelnuts, toasted and finely ground

1 tablespoon unsalted butter, melted

confectioners' sugar, for dusting

FILLING

¼ cup crème fraîche, whipped

1 cup raspberries

a 12 x 8 x 1 inch jelly roll pan, greased and lined with parchment paper

SERVES 6–8

Preheat the oven to 400°F. Put the eggs and sugar in a large bowl and, using an electric hand-mixer, whisk until pale, thick, and creamy. The mixture should leave a ribbonlike trail on the surface when lifted. Using a large metal spoon, fold in the flour and hazelnuts. Drizzle the melted butter over the surface of the mixture, then fold it in carefully.

Pour the mixture into the prepared jelly roll pan and level the surface. Bake in the preheated oven for 15–20 minutes until golden and the sponge springs back when lightly pressed with the tips of your fingers.

Remove from the oven and turn out onto parchment paper sprinkled with sugar. Peel off the lining paper and trim the edges of the roulade. Roll up the sponge from the short end with the paper inside. Let cool.

When ready to fill, gently unroll the sponge and remove the paper. Spread with a layer of crème fraîche, add the raspberries, and roll up as before. Dust with confectioners' sugar, then slice and serve.

An extra-special treat for chocaholics—made even more indulgent when served with lots of whipped cream and fresh cherries. Use good-quality chocolate for maximum flavor.

Chocolate truffle cake

Preheat the oven to 350°F. Melt the chocolate in a heatproof bowl set over a saucepan of barely simmering water (don't let the bowl touch the water). When just melted, remove from the heat and stir in the cocoa. Mix well and let cool until lukewarm.

Using an electric hand-mixer, whisk the eggs, sugar, and cornstarch until pale and doubled in volume. Using a large metal spoon, fold in the cooled chocolate, then the cream.

Pour the mixture into the prepared cake pan and bake in the preheated oven for about 1 hour or until a toothpick inserted into the center comes out clean.

Remove from the oven and run a sharp knife around the edge of the pan. Let cool in the pan (the cake will sink a little in the middle).

Remove from the pan and dust with confectioners' sugar. To serve, cut into slices and add cream and cherries, if using.

8 oz. bittersweet chocolate

¼ cup unsweetened cocoa, sifted

4 eggs, lightly beaten

½ cup confectioners' sugar, sifted, plus extra for dusting

1 tablespoon cornstarch

⅔ cup heavy cream, lightly whipped

TO SERVE

lightly whipped cream

fresh cherries, pitted (optional)

a springform cake pan, 8 inches diameter, greased and lined with parchment paper

SERVES 6–8

BASE

4 tablespoons unsalted butter

3½ oz graham crackers, crushed into fine crumbs

FIRST LAYER

two 8-oz. packages cream cheese

2 large eggs

½ cup sugar

¼ teaspoon pure vanilla extract

SECOND LAYER

1¼ cups sour cream

⅔ cup thick Greek-style yogurt

2½ tablespoons sugar

1 teaspoon pure vanilla extract

BLUEBERRY TOPPING

¼ cup sugar

8 oz. blueberries

1 teaspoon arrowroot

a springform cake pan, 8 inches diameter

SERVES 8–10

This is a favorite cheesecake recipe, and goes down a treat after a light meal or as a naughty afternoon bite.

Blueberry cheesecake

Preheat the oven to 375°F. Gently melt the butter in a saucepan, let cool slightly, and add the crushed crackers. Press evenly into the base of the cake pan.

Beat the ingredients for the first layer together thoroughly, pour over the base and smooth the top. Put the pan on a baking sheet and bake in the oven for 20 minutes or until just set. Set aside for 20 minutes to firm up. Mix the ingredients for the second layer and spoon evenly over the first layer. Return to the oven for 10 minutes then take out and let cool. Refrigerate for at least 6 hours or overnight.

For the topping, heat the sugar gently with 2 tablespoons water until it dissolves. Turn up the heat, add the blueberries, cover, and cook for 5 minutes, shaking the pan occasionally until the berries are soft. Take off the heat. Mix the arrowroot with 2 tablespoons water and add to the blueberries. Stir over a gentle heat until the juice has thickened. Set aside to cool. Check for sweetness and add extra sugar to taste. An hour before serving, ease a knife down the side of the cake pan, then release the clamp and remove the sides. Spoon the topping over the cheesecake and return to the refrigerator until ready to serve.

Family Favorites

Sometimes it's the plain cakes that are the best. This one is wonderfully buttery and zesty and is delicious served simply—cut into elegant fingers or squares. To achieve a really crisp, sugary crust on top, combine the sugar and lemon juice at the last minute and pour straight over the cake before letting it cool.

Lemon drizzle cake

5 oz. butter, at room temperature

⅔ cup sugar

2 large eggs

grated zest of 1 unwaxed lemon

1 cup plus 1 tablespoon self-rising flour

LEMON TOPPING

4 tablespoons sugar

freshly squeezed juice of 1 unwaxed lemon

an 8-inch square cake pan with a removable bottom, base-lined with parchment paper

SERVES 8–10

Preheat the oven to 350°F. Beat together the butter and sugar in a bowl until pale and creamy. Beat in the eggs, one at a time, then stir in the lemon zest. Sift the flour into the mixture and fold in until well mixed. Transfer the mixture into the prepared cake pan and spread evenly.

Bake in the preheated oven for about 20 minutes until risen and golden and a skewer inserted in the center comes out clean.

Transfer the cake pan to a wire rack and prick the top of the cake all over using the skewer. Dust with 1 tablespoon of the sugar for the topping.

Quickly combine the remaining sugar and lemon juice in a small bowl and immediately pour over the top of the cake. Let cool in the pan, then carefully unmold to serve.

*One of the most popular after-dinner desserts, who
could forget Key Lime Pie? Its tangy sweetness is
refreshingly indulgent, and will take you back to lazy
summer afternoons spent with friends and family.*

Key lime pie

Roll out the dough and use to line the tart pan. Bake blind
following the method given on page 60. Reduce the oven
to 350°F.

To make the lime filling, put 1 whole egg and 3 egg yolks
in a bowl and beat until blended. Whisk in the condensed
milk and lime zest. Gradually whisk in the lime juice.

Put the egg whites and cream of tartar in a separate, grease-
free bowl and whisk until stiff but not dry. Beat 2 tablespoons
of egg white mixture into the egg yolk mixture, then fold
in the remainder with a spatula. Spoon into the pie crust
and bake in the preheated oven for 20 minutes or until
risen and just firm in the center. Remove from the oven and
let cool in the pan on a wire rack. It will deflate as it cools.

When cool, make the topping. Put the cream and
2 tablespoons of the sugar in a bowl, whip until softly
stiff, then spread over the lime filling. Toss the shreds of
lime zest in the remaining sugar and use to decorate the
tart. Serve cold but not chilled.

**1 RECIPE SWEET TART
PASTRY DOUGH (*SEE*
PAGE 60)**

LIME FILLING

4 eggs, 3 of them separated

one 14-oz. can sweetened
condensed milk

2 tablespoons grated
unwaxed lime zest

½ cup plus 1 tablespoon
freshly squeezed lime juice

¼ teaspoon cream of tartar

CREAM TOPPING

1 cup whipping cream

3 tablepoons vanilla sugar

zest of 1 large unwaxed
lime, pared into fine shreds

**a tart pan, 10 inches
diameter**

SERVES 6–8

*A scrumptious family treat—who doesn't remember
enjoying a delicious slice of carrot cake as a child?
A sprinkling of orange zest in this recipe adds a
touch of tanginess to the sweet frosting.*

Carrot cake

4 eggs, separated

1 cup packed brown sugar

zest and juice of 1 unwaxed
orange

1⅔ cups ground walnuts

1 teaspoon ground cinnamon

1½ cups grated carrot

¾ cup whole-wheat flour

1 teaspoon baking powder

FROSTING

8 oz. cream cheese

⅔ cup confectioners' sugar

zest and juice of 1 small
unwaxed orange

**an 8-inch square cake
pan with a removable
bottom, greased**

SERVES 8–10

Preheat the oven to 350°F. Put the egg yolks and sugar
in a bowl and whisk until thick and creamy. Add all the
remaining ingredients except the egg whites, and fold
carefully until the mixture is smooth.

Whisk the egg whites until stiff, then fold into the cake
mixture. Pour into the prepared cake pan and bake in the
center of the preheated oven for 1 hour. When done, let
cool in the pan for 5 minutes, then turn out and cool
completely on a wire rack.

To make the frosting, beat the cream cheese and
confectioners' sugar together. Add a little orange zest
and enough juice to flavor. Spread over the top of the
cold cake using a narrow spatula dipped in hot water.
Sprinkle with the remaining orange zest before serving.

Pumpkin pie

Pumpkin Pie is traditionally served at Thanksgiving, but makes a great after-dinner dessert for all the family. Butternut squash purée is an acceptable substitute if pumpkin is not available.

Preheat the oven to 325°F. Cut the pumpkin into large chunks and bake in the preheated oven for about 1 hour. Scrape the flesh from the skin and purée until smooth in a food processor. Raise the oven to 375°F.

Bring the dough to room temperature. Roll out the dough thinly on a lightly floured work surface, then use to line the tart pans or pie plates. Trim and crimp or decorate the edges as you wish. Prick the bases all over with a fork, chill or freeze for 15 minutes, then bake blind following the method given on page 61.

Lower the oven to 325°F.

Put all the filling ingredients into a food processor and blend until smooth. Pour into the pie crusts, set on a baking sheet and bake for about 1 hour or until just set. Remove from the oven and let stand for 10 minutes, then remove the tart pan and let cool for a few minutes. Serve warm or at room temperature, not chilled.

1 RECIPE AMERICAN PIE CRUST DOUGH (*SEE* PAGE 61)

PUMPKIN FILLING

1 pumpkin or butternut squash

½ cup light brown sugar

3 extra large eggs

¾ cup evaporated milk, about 7 oz.

½ cup light corn syrup

a good pinch of salt

1 teaspoon ground cinnamon

½ teaspoon nutmeg

1 teaspoon vanilla extract

2 tablespoons rum (optional)

2 tart pans or pie plates, 9 inches diameter

SERVES 12

**1 RECIPE SWEET TART
PASTRY DOUGH
(*SEE* PAGE 60)**

LEMON FILLING

1 large egg and 3 large
eggs yolks

½ cup sugar

finely grated zest and
freshly squeezed juice of
2 large unwaxed lemons

1 stick unsalted butter,
melted and cooled

½ cup whipping cream

MERINGUE

3 large egg whites

¼ teaspoon cream of tartar

½ cup sugar, plus
1 tablespoon for sprinkling

½ teaspoon finely grated
lemon zest

**a loose-bottomed
tart pan, 9–10 inches
diameter**

SERVES 6–8

*For some of us, one of our earliest cooking memories as
a child must be making this classic dessert. The buttery,
lemony filling for this pie is a delight, and the cloud of
fluffy, crisp-crusted meringue is mandatory for any
Lemon Meringue Pie worthy of the name.*

Lemon meringue pie

Roll out the dough and use to line the tart pan. Bake blind
(*see* page 61). Lower the oven to 325°F.

To make the filling, put the egg, egg yolks, and sugar in a
bowl and beat until slightly thickened and a paler yellow.
Beat in the lemon zest, butter, cream, and finally the
lemon juice. Pour the filling into the pie crust and bake
in the preheated oven for 20–30 minutes until the filling
is barely set in the center. Do not let it overbake.

To make the meringue, put the egg whites and cream of
tartar in a grease-free bowl and, using an electric whisk,
whisk until frothy and the whisk leaves stiff peaks. Whisk
in half the sugar until the meringue is thick and glossy. Fold in
the remaining sugar and the lemon zest using a metal spoon.
Pile the meringue onto the tart, swirling and peaking as
you go. Sprinkle with the 1 tablespoon sugar and return the
tart to the oven for 30–35 minutes or until the meringue is
browned and crisp on the outside. Serve just warm or cold.

Teatime

Traditionally served with clotted cream and rich, fruity jam, these classic scones are a must for the tea table—a typically British treat.

Scones with clotted cream and strawberry jam

1¼ cup self-rising flour

1 teaspoon baking powder

2 tablespoons sugar

3 tablespoons plus
1 teaspoon unsalted
butter, chilled and diced

1 egg

⅓ cup milk

TO SERVE

clotted cream or extra-thick heavy cream

good-quality strawberry jam

a cookie cutter, 2 inches diameter

a baking sheet, greased

MAKES 10–12

Preheat the oven to 425°F. Put the flour, baking powder, and sugar in a food processor and pulse to combine. Add the butter and process for about 20 seconds until the mixture resembles fine bread crumbs. Transfer to a large bowl and make a well in the center.

Beat together the egg and milk in another bowl, reserving 1 tablespoon of the mixture in a separate bowl. Pour most of the remaining liquid into the flour mixture and bring together into a soft dough using a fork. If there are still dry crumbs, add more of the liquid. Turn out onto a floured surface and knead until smooth. Gently pat or roll out the dough to about 1 inch thick and cut out rounds using the cookie cutter, using the trimmings to make more scones.

Arrange the scones on the prepared baking sheet, spacing them apart, and brush the tops with the reserved egg and milk mixture. Bake in the preheated oven for 8 minutes until risen and golden. Transfer to a wire rack to cool slightly. Serve warm with the cream and strawberry jam.

Macaroons

Macaroons come in many varieties, and make an excellent teatime treat if you fancy something a little sweet. Crisp on the outside and chewy in the middle, these delicate fancies are perfect for balancing on the edge of your saucer.

Preheat the oven to 350°F. Scatter the pistachio nuts on the unlined baking sheet and bake in the preheated oven for about 3 minutes. Pour onto a clean paper towel and rub together to remove the brown papery skins. Put the pistachios and confectioners' sugar in a food processor and process until finely ground.

Put the egg whites in a clean bowl and whisk to form stiff peaks. Sprinkle the pistachio mixture over the top and gently fold into the mixture. Spoon the mixture into the piping bag and pipe 1-inch rounds onto the lined baking sheets, spacing them slightly apart. Bake in the preheated oven for 10–12 minutes until light golden. Let cool slightly, then carefully remove using a palette knife and transfer to a wire rack to cool completely.

To serve, stir the mascarpone into the chocolate until well blended, then use to sandwich the macaroons together.

¼ cup shelled pistachio nuts

½ cup plus 1 tablespoon confectioners' sugar

2 egg whites

1½ tablespoons mascarpone

½ oz. dark chocolate, melted and cooled slightly

a piping bag fitted with a ½-inch round tip

3 baking sheets, 2 lined with parchment paper

MAKES ABOUT 16

Muffins are quick and easy to prepare and make a lovely brunch snack, especially when served warm with coffee. Blueberries make a delicious muffin, but you could replace them with raspberries if you prefer.

Warm blueberry and almond muffins

1¾ cups all-purpose flour

1½ teaspoons baking powder

1 teaspoon apple pie spice

½ cup ground almonds or ¾ cup slivered almonds, finely ground in a food processor

¾ cup sugar

1 egg

1¼ cups buttermilk

4 tablespoons butter, melted

8 oz. blueberries

2 tablespoons almonds, chopped

a 12-cup muffin pan, lined with 10 paper muffin cups

MAKES 10

Preheat the oven to 400°F. Sift the flour, baking powder, and apple pie spice into a bowl and stir in the ground almonds and sugar. Put the egg, buttermilk, and melted butter in a second bowl and beat well. Stir into the dry ingredients to make a smooth batter.

Fold in the blueberries, then spoon the mixture into the paper muffin cups in the muffin pan until three-quarters full. Scatter with the chopped almonds and bake in the preheated oven for 18–20 minutes until risen and golden. Remove from the oven, let cool slightly on a wire rack, and serve warm.

Walnut tart and taffy ice cream

This soft, sticky tart packed with walnuts is superb with the easy vanilla ice cream marbled with taffy.

Bring the dough to room temperature. Preheat the oven to 375°F. Roll out the dough on a lightly floured work surface and use to line the tart pan. Prick the base, chill or freeze for 15 minutes, then bake blind following the method given on page 61. Cool. Lower the oven to 350°F.

To make the filling, put the butter and sugar into a bowl and cream until light and fluffy. Gradually beat in the eggs, one at a time. Beat the orange zest and juice into the butter and egg mixture. Heat the light corn syrup in a small saucepan until runny, but not very hot. Stir into the butter mixture, then stir in the walnuts and salt. Pour into the pie crust and bake for 45 minutes until lightly browned and risen. The tart will sink a little on cooling.

While the tart is cooling, make the ice cream. Put the taffy and cream into a small saucepan and stir over medium heat to melt. Cool slightly and stir quickly into the ice cream so that it looks marbled. Put the ice cream back in the freezer until ready to serve. Serve the tart at room temperature with scoops of the taffy ice cream.

1 RECIPE SWEET RICH SHORTCRUST PASTRY DOUGH (*SEE* PAGE 56)

WALNUT FILLING

1¼ sticks unsalted butter, softened

½ cup plus 2 tablespoons light brown sugar

3 extra large eggs

grated zest and juice of 1 small unwaxed orange

¾ cup light corn syrup

8 oz. walnut halves (2½ cups), coarsely chopped

a pinch of salt

QUICK TAFFY ICE CREAM

6 oz. taffy

½ cup heavy cream

1 pint best-quality vanilla ice cream, softened

a fluted tart pan, 9 inches diameter

SERVES 6

Ever popular and hard to beat, chocolate chip cookies have always been a childhood favorite. This classic recipe uses less sugar and more nuts than most. Use plain chocolate broken up into chunks or a bag of choc chips.

Classic choc chip cookies

1⅓ cups self-rising flour

a pinch of salt

a good pinch of baking soda

1 stick unsalted butter, very soft

⅓ cup minus 1 tablespoon sugar

⅓ cup lightly packed light brown sugar

½ teaspoon pure vanilla extract

1 extra large egg, lightly beaten

1 cup semi-sweet chocolate chips

¼ cup walnut or pecan pieces

2 baking sheets, greased

MAKES 24

Preheat the oven to 375°F. Put all the ingredients in a large bowl and mix thoroughly with a wooden spoon.

Drop heaping teaspoons of the mixture onto the prepared baking sheets, spacing them well apart.

Bake in the preheated oven for 8–10 minutes until lightly colored and just firm.

Let cool on the sheets for a minute, then transfer to a wire rack to cool completely.

Store in an airtight container and eat within 5 days or freeze for up to a month.

Sweet rich shortcrust pastry dough

This is a wonderfully light and crumbly pastry. It is best used for richer pies and tarts, or where the shell is more than just a carrier for the filling and the taste of the pastry is important. It can be made in a food processor, but the classic method gives a slightly lighter result— and besides, there is something satisfying about making pastry by hand.

USE FOR CLASSIC LEMON TART (PAGE 14) AND WALNUT TART (PAGE 53)

2 cups all-purpose flour, plus extra for dusting

½ teaspoon salt

2 tablespoons confectioners' sugar

9 tablespoons unsalted butter, chilled and diced

2 large egg yolks

2 tablespoons ice water

MAKES 14 OZ. PASTRY DOUGH, enough to line the base of a 10-inch tart pan or make a double crust for a deep, 8-inch pie plate

1 Sift the flour, salt, and confectioners' sugar together into a bowl, then rub in the butter.

2 Mix the egg yolks with the ice water. Add to the flour, mixing lightly with a knife.
Note The dough must have some water in it or it will be too difficult to handle. If it is still too dry, add a little more water, sprinkling it over the flour mixture 1 tablespoon at a time.

3 Invert the mixture onto a lightly floured work surface.

4 Knead lightly with your hands until smooth.

5 Form the dough into a rough ball.

6 Flatten slightly, wrap in plastic wrap, and chill for at least 30 minutes before rolling out.

Pâte brisée

This dough is really the French version of an unsweetened shortcrust. It has a finer texture so should be rolled out much thinner—to about ⅛ inch. Sometimes unsweetened pâte brisée is used for fruit tarts that are baked for a long time, because other pastries with a high sugar content would scorch before the fruit was cooked. This dough provides a firm, crisp support for the fruit. Don't be tempted to leave out the water—it makes the dough stronger and easier to handle in the end.

USE FOR FRESH RASPBERRY TART (PAGE 18)

1½ cups all-purpose flour, plus extra for dusting

a large pinch of salt

8 tablespoons (1 stick) unsalted butter, diced, at room temperature

1 large egg yolk

2½–3 tablespoons ice water

MAKES ABOUT 12 OZ. PASTRY DOUGH, enough to line a 10-inch tart pan, or 6 x 3-inch tartlet pans

1-2 Sift the flour and salt into a mound on a clean work surface. Make a well in the middle with your fist.

3 Put the butter and egg yolk into the well and, using the fingers of one hand, "peck" the eggs and butter together until they look like scrambled eggs.

4 Using a spatula or pastry scraper, flick the flour over the egg mixture and chop through until almost incorporated.

5 Sprinkle with the water, and chop again.

6 Bring together quickly with your hands. Knead lightly into a ball, then flatten slightly. Wrap in plastic wrap and chill for at least 30 minutes. Let it return to room temperature before rolling out.

Sweet tart pastry dough

This pastry is easily made in a food processor and creates a crisp, biscuity crust.

USE FOR KEY LIME PIE (PAGE 37) AND LEMON MERINGUE PIE (PAGE 42)

1⅓ cups all-purpose flour

a pinch of salt

⅓ cup confectioners' sugar

6 tablespoons unsalted butter, chilled and cut into small cubes

1 large egg, separated

1½–2 tablespoons cold lemon juice or ice water

MAKES 1 TART CASE
a loose-based tart pan, 9–10 inches diameter, 1–2 inches deep

1 Put the flour, salt, confectioners' sugar, and butter in a food processor fitted with a metal blade. Process until the ingredients are thoroughly mixed and the mixture has a sandy appearance. Add the egg yolk and 1½ tablespoons of the lemon juice and process again until the dough forms a ball and leaves the side of the bowl. Add extra lemon juice if the dough seems dry and crumbly.

2 Form the dough into a ball, pressing it gently to get rid of cracks, wrap in foil, and chill for 1 hour. Remove from the refrigerator and let the dough soften for 10–15 minutes at room temperature before rolling out. Put the dough on a lightly floured work surface and roll it out fairly thinly. Use it to line the tart pan, making sure you ease the dough into the corners without stretching it. Trim off the excess pastry.

3 To blind bake the tart case, take long, thin strips of foil and fold them over the edge of the tart, to protect and support the sides of the pastry case. Prick the base of the tart all over with a fork. Chill for 30–40 minutes.

4 Bake the tart case in a preheated oven at 375°F for 8–10 minutes until lightly colored. Beat the egg white with a fork to break it up. Remove the foil strips and brush the tart case with egg white. Return to the oven for 8–10 minutes or until the pastry is golden and crisp. Let the tart case cool in the pan before unmolding.

This American pie crust recipe dough is enough to make two pies.

1 Sift the flour and salt into a large bowl. Cut in the shortening using 2 round-bladed knives or a pastry blender (or do this in a food processor).

2 Beat the egg in a separate bowl. Stir the vinegar or lemon juice into the egg, then add the water.

3 Pour the wet mixture into the dry mixture, then cut it in with the knives or pastry blender again. Bring the dough together quickly, using your hands. Knead until smooth, either in the bowl or on a floured work surface. Divide in 2 so it is easier to roll out later.

4 Shape the 2 balls of dough into flattened balls, wrap in plastic wrap, then chill for at least 30 minutes before rolling out.

Baking blind

Preheat the oven to 400°F. Line the pastry case with foil, then fill with beans. Set on a baking sheet and bake in the center of the oven for about 10–12 minutes. Remove the foil and the baking beans and return the pastry case to the oven for a further 5–7 minutes to dry out completely. To prevent pastry from becoming soggy from the filling, brush the blind-baked case with beaten egg. Bake again for 5–10 minutes until set and shiny. This will also seal any holes made when pricking before the blind baking.

American pie crust dough

USE FOR PUMPKIN PIE (PAGE 41)

2¼ cups all-purpose flour, plus extra for dusting

a good pinch of salt

1⅓ cups vegetable shortening, chilled

1 large egg

1 tablespoon wine vinegar or lemon juice

¼ cup ice water

MAKES ABOUT 1½ LB. PASTRY DOUGH, enough for 2 single deep pie crusts, 9 inches diameter

Sweet shortcrust pastry dough

This sweet shortcrust pastry is ideal for fruit tarts. Its high sugar content means it can burn very easily, so use a timer.

1 Put the flour and butter into a food processor and process until the mixture looks like bread crumbs. Add the sugar and process briefly.

2 With the machine running, gradually add 3 egg yolks until the mixture comes together to form a ball. (Add the extra egg yolk if it is too dry.)

3 Transfer the pastry to a lightly floured surface and knead very gently with your hands until smooth.

4 Divide in half, wrap each piece in plastic wrap and chill for 40 minutes.

USE FOR BLACKBERRY AND APPLE PIE (PAGE 10)

2⅓ cups all-purpose flour

2 sticks butter, cut into small pieces

½ cup (minus 1 tablespoon) sugar

3–4 egg yolks

Index

Conversion chart

Weights and measures have been rounded up or down slightly to make measuring easier.

The recipes in this book require the following conversions:

American	Metric	Imperial
6 tbsp	85 g	3 oz
7 tbsp	100 g	3½ oz
1 stick	115 g	4 oz

Measuring butter:
A US stick of butter weighs 4 oz which is approximately 115 g or 8 tablespoons.

Volume equivalents:

American	Metric	Imperial
1 teaspoon	5 ml	
1 tablespoon	15 ml	
¼ cup	60 ml	2 fl oz
⅓ cup	75 ml	2½ fl oz
½ cup	125 ml	4 fl oz
⅔ cup	150 ml	5 fl oz (¼ pint)
¾ cup	175 ml	6 fl oz
1 cup	250 ml	8 fl oz

Oven temperatures:

120°C	(250°F)	Gas ½
140°C	(275°F)	Gas 1
150°C	(300°F)	Gas 2
170°C	(325°F)	Gas 3
180°C	(350°F)	Gas 4
190°C	(375°F)	Gas 5
200°C	(400°F)	Gas 6
220°C	(425°F)	Gas 7

Weight equivalents:

Imperial	Metric
1 oz	30 g
2 oz	55 g
3 oz	85 g
3½ oz	100 g
4 oz	115 g
6 oz	175 g
8 oz (½ lb)	225 g
9 oz	250 g
10 oz	280 g
12 oz	350 g
13 oz	375 g
14 oz	400 g
15 oz	425 g
16 oz (1 lb)	450 g

Measurements:

Inches	cm
¼ inch	5 mm
½ inch	1 cm
1 inch	2.5 cm
2 inches	5 cm
3 inches	7 cm
4 inches	10 cm
5 inches	12 cm
6 inches	15 cm
7 inches	18 cm
8 inches	20 cm
9 inches	23 cm
10 inches	25 cm
11 inches	28 cm
12 inches	30 cm

Credits